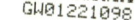

Strong MIND

Dedicated to
Venerable
Wangdor
Rimpoche

Written by Ziji Rinpoche
& Niko, a 6 year old boy
www.shortmomentsforkids.com

Illustrated by
Celine Wright
BeginningMind Series #2

Copyright © 2020 Short Moments for Kids

All rights reserved.

No part of this publication may be reproduced or distributed in any form without prior written consent from the publisher.

Text © 2020 Ziji Rinpoche
Illustrations and cover design © 2020 Celine Wright
2nd edition © 2020 Celine Wright

Book #2 of the BeginningMind Series
Hardback ISBN: 978-1-915175-10-6
Paperback ISBN: 978-1-915175-05-2
Ebook ISBN: 978-1-915175-14-4
http://shortmomentsforkids.com

Short Moments of Strong Mind
for Kids

Dedicated to... you!

Practice strong mind when you have stormy feelings
because strong mind is always happy, calm
and has very powerful kindness.
Strong mind is always available to help you.
Strong mind belongs to you and no one can take it away!
It belongs to you!

Mind is kind. Mind is loving.
Mind is always strong and smart.

When we rely on strong mind, our kindness and powerful energy grow.

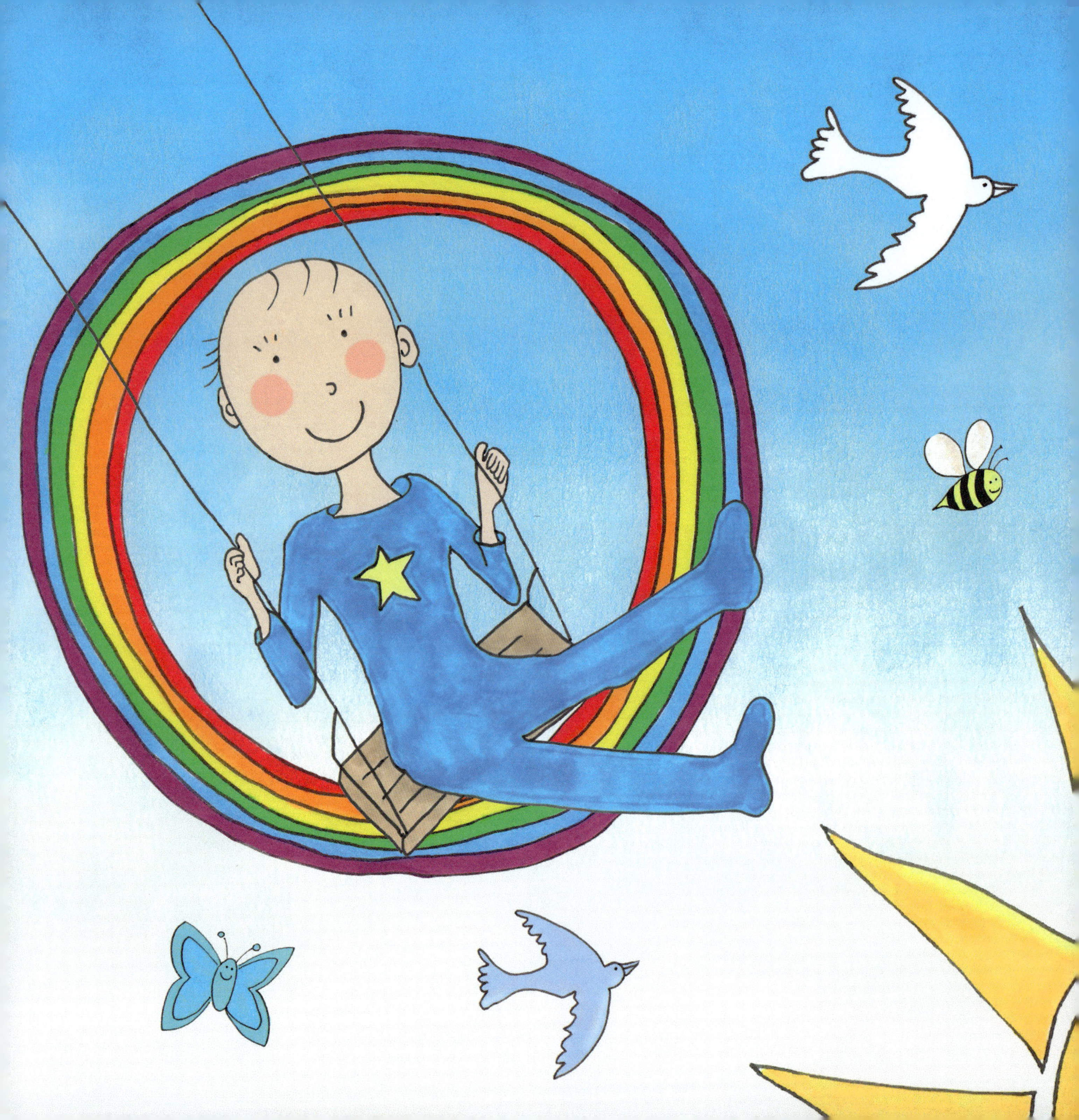

Strong mind is happy
like sunshine
in the sky.

How do you know what to do with your body?

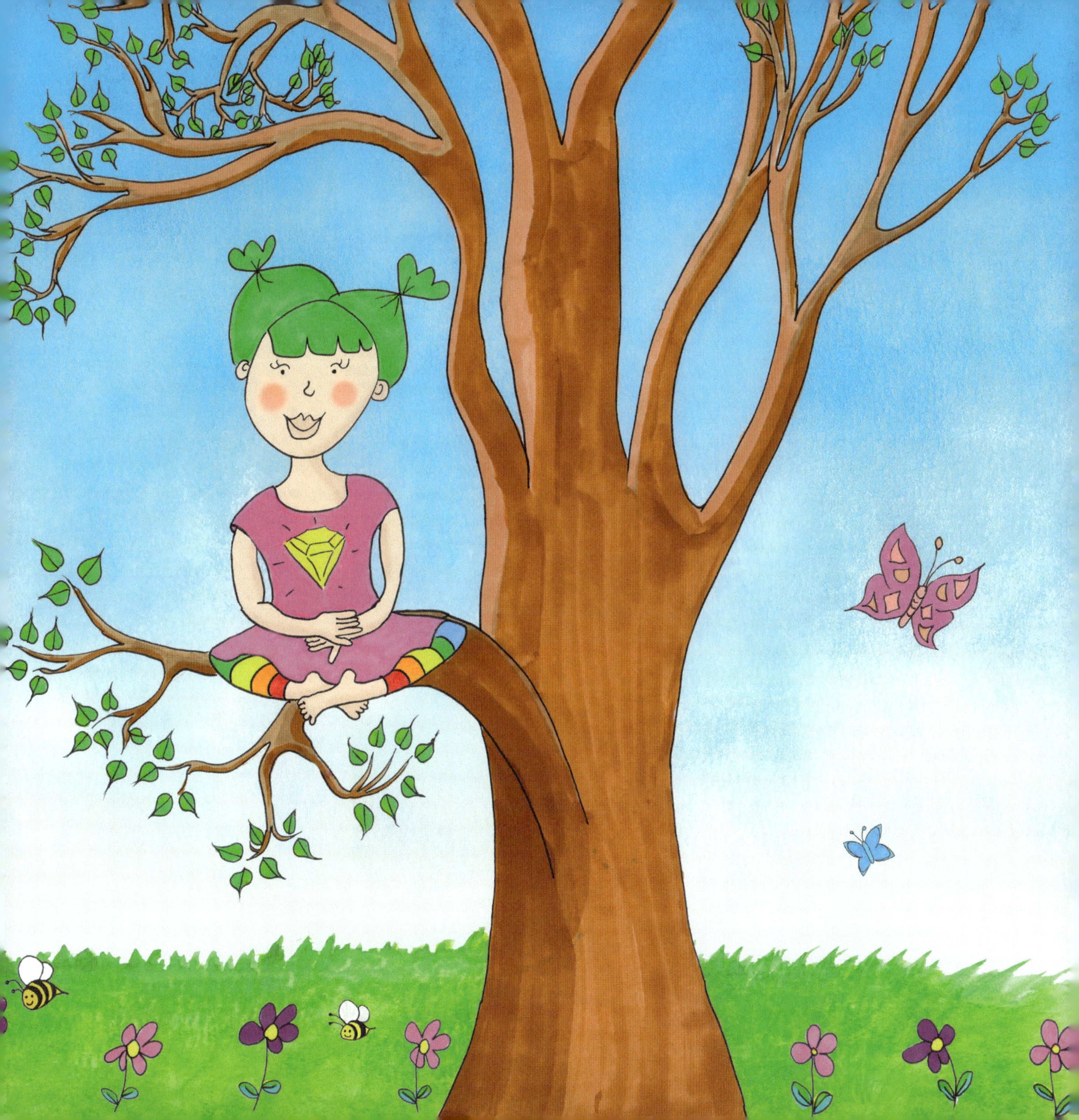

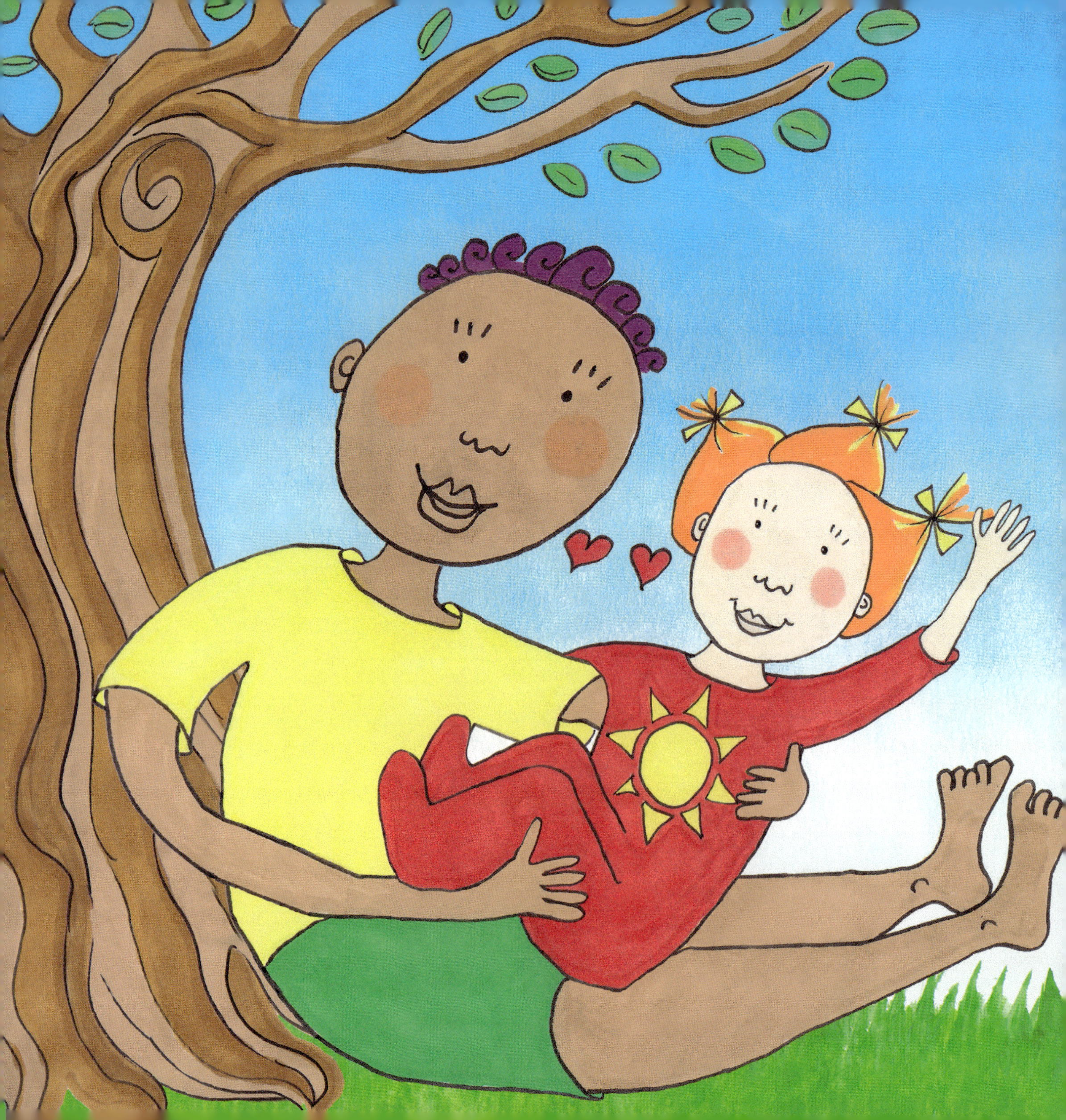

How do you know the words to say when you talk?

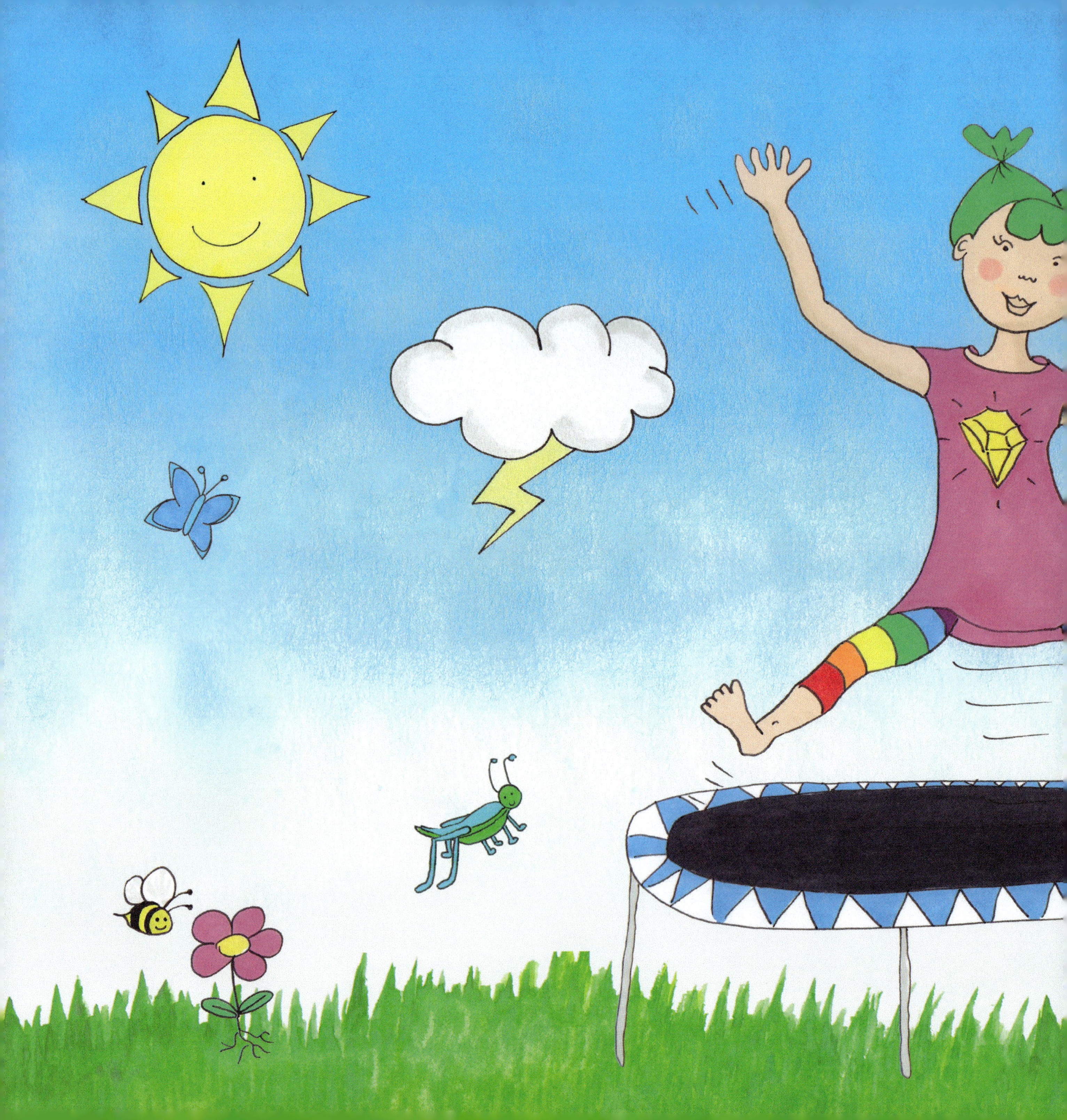

AHA!

Mind tells body
what to do.

Mind tells speech
what to do.

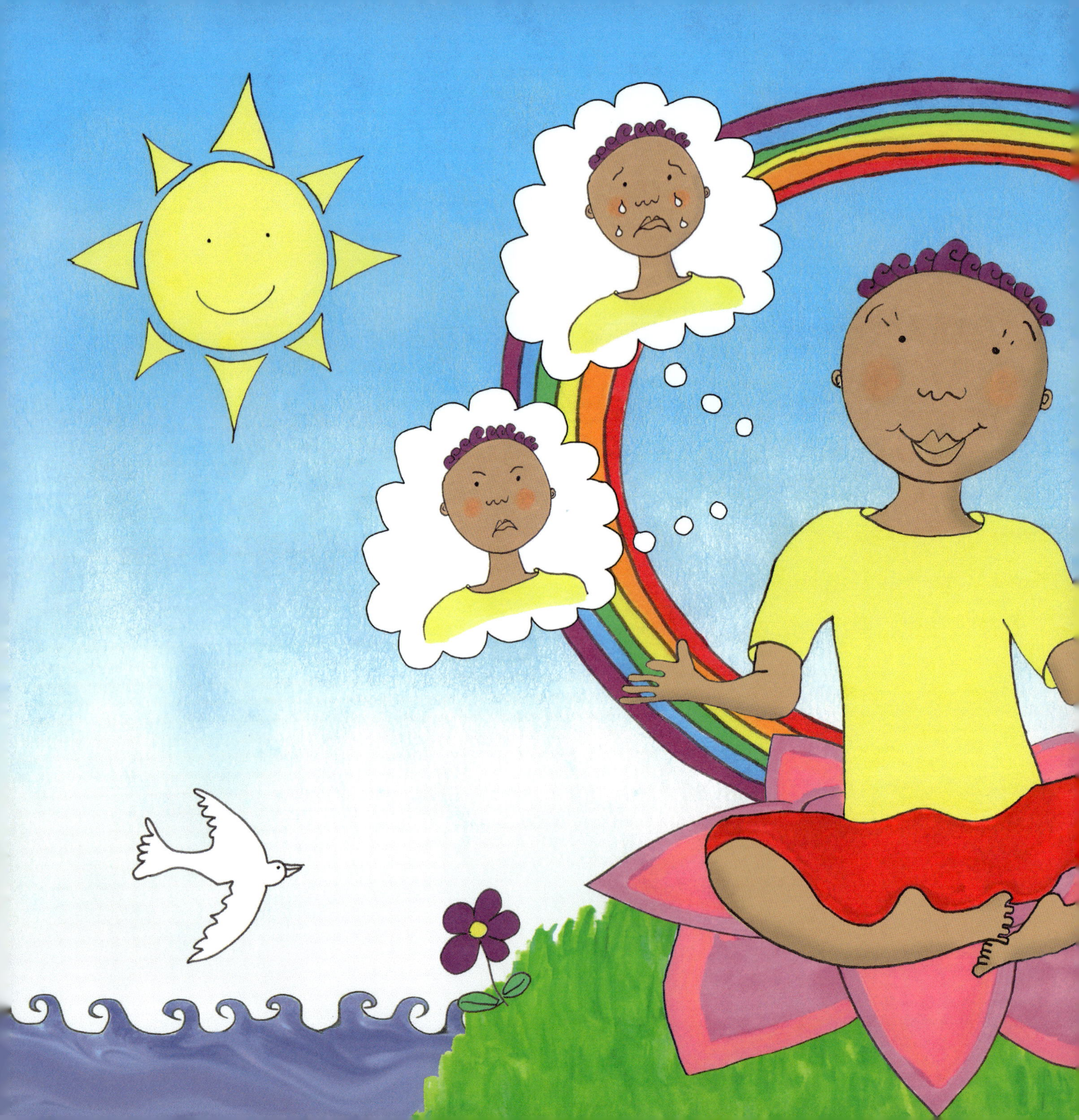

Mind tells thoughts and feelings what to do.

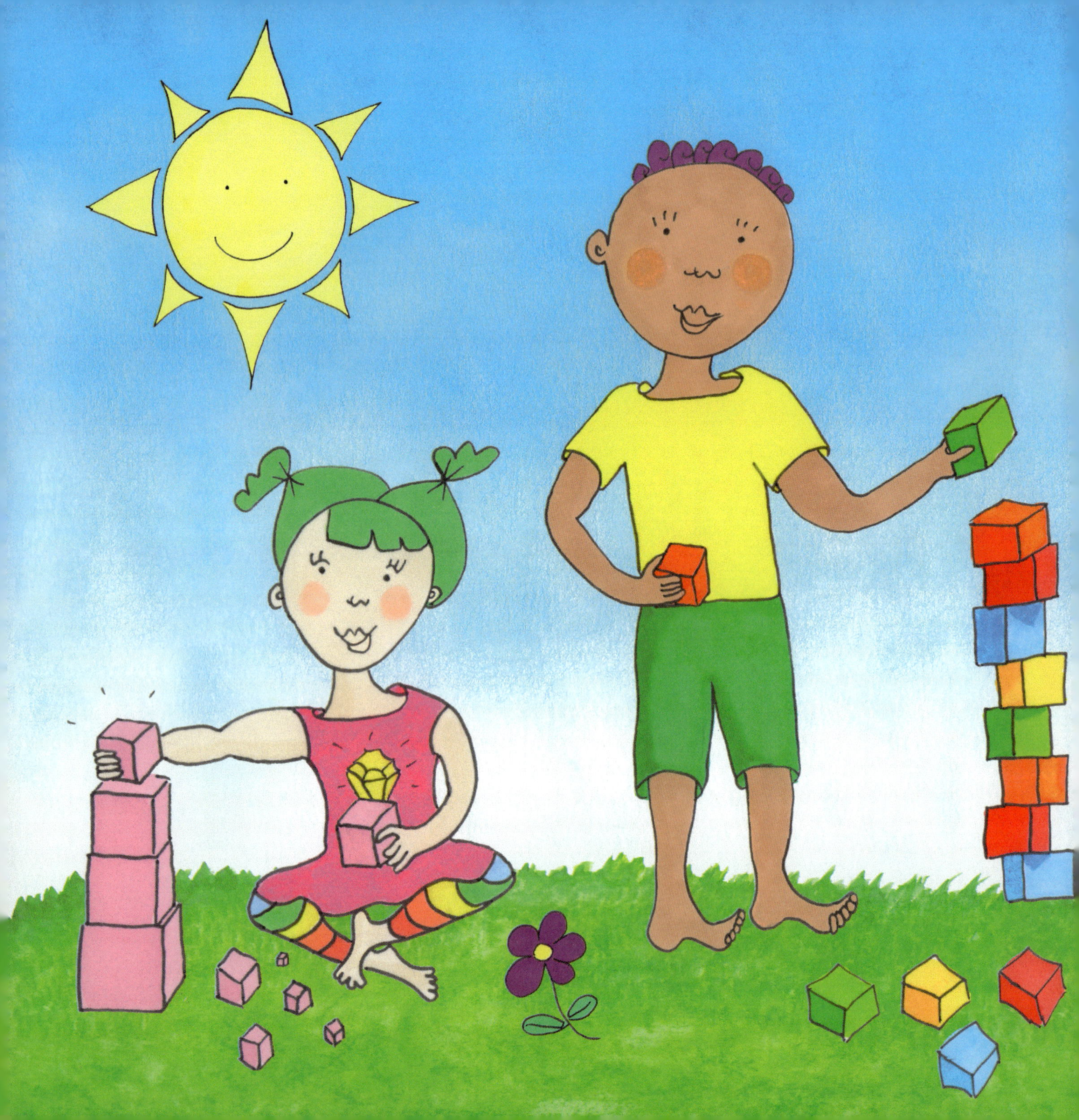

Hey!
Thoughts and feelings cannot tell our mind what to do.

Can birds tell the sky what to do?

No! Birds cannot tell the sky what to do.

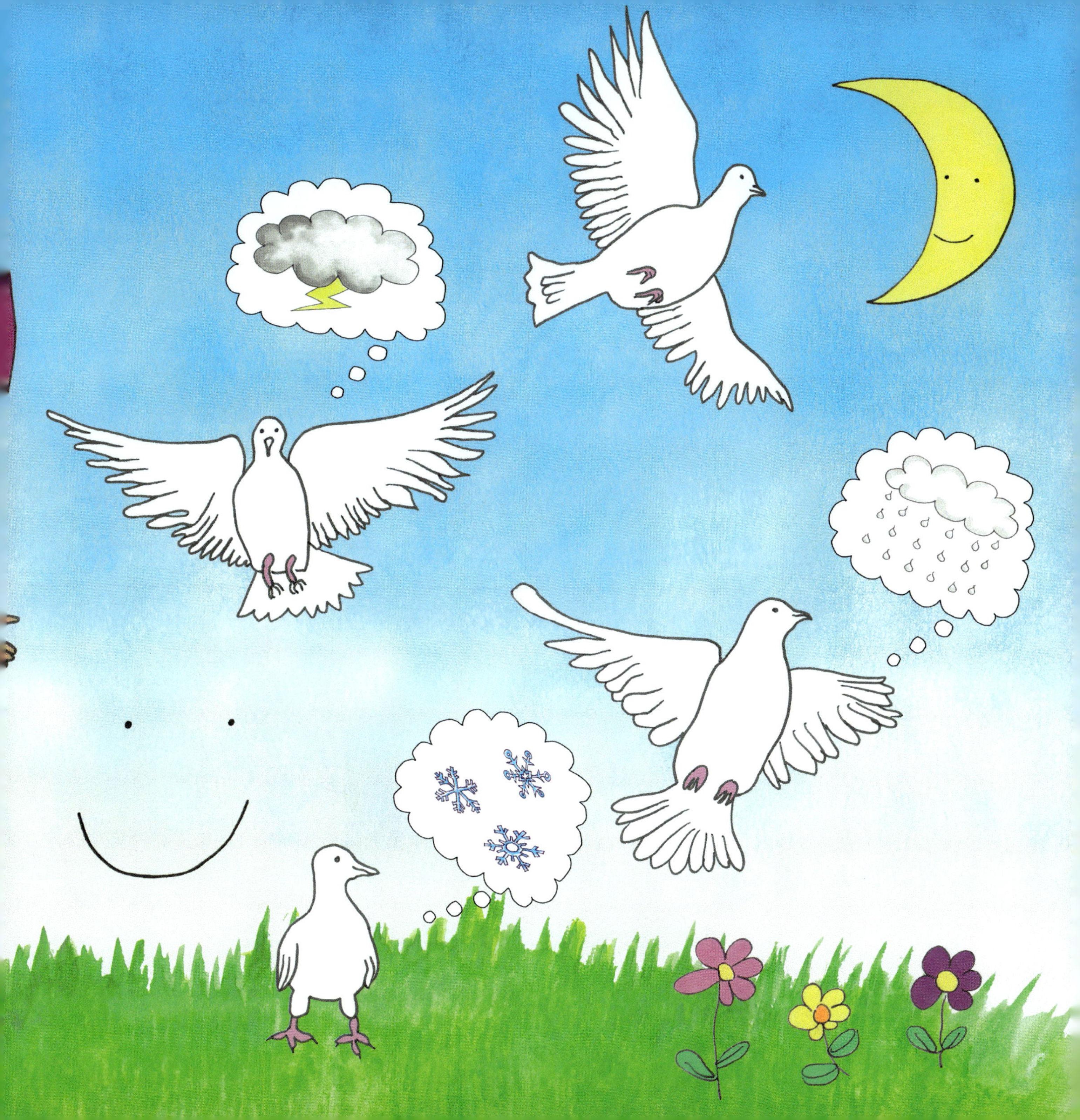

And thoughts and feelings cannot tell our mind what to do.

Our thoughts and feelings fly on by
like a bird in the sky, they leave no trace.

Hmmm, speaking of stormy feelings,
where are stormy feelings?
Let's look. Are stormy feelings...

In your back?

In your big toe?

In your hand?

No!

The mind is strong and calm like the sky.
Stormy feelings are like a rainbow in the sky.

Just as a rainbow quickly disappears,
stormy feelings disappear too.

Strong mind is kind
and completely filled...

...with powerful energy.

Your strong mind is completely filled with happiness!

The author Ziji Rinpoche and her teacher Wangdor Rimpoche

Ziji Rinpoche loves to teach and write and her latest book is called 'When Surfing a Tsunami...' Ziji Rinpoche is the Dzogchen Lineage successor of Venerable Wangdor Rimpoche. Each metaphor and key instruction originate from Dzogchen teachings which were passed down from one teacher to another, like a chain of golden mountains. Wangdor Rimpoche asked Ziji Rinpoche to bring about the furtherance of Dzogchen within contemporary global culture. Ziji Rinpoche established the Short Moments online community for mutual support in gaining familiarity with the nature of mind. Through the Short Moments app, anyone can access profound and powerful Dzogchen teachings. Find out more on http://shortmoments.com

The illustrator Celine Wright

Celine loves to draw, empower children and tell stories. When she was introduced to the nature of mind by Ziji Rinpoche, she was awestruck at the power of mind, open like the sky, always clear and wise no matter the stormy feelings. She recognized she would have loved to learn about mind as a child. She was inspired to illustrate the teachings in children's books introducing strong mind to kids. Combining her training in Fine Arts (BA), Performing Arts (MA), Dzogchen (Student of Ziji Rinpoche since 2007) and Early Years (Childminder), Celine now teaches Dzogchen for Kids, conducts book readings in schools and festivals and loves to illustrate new books at http://shortmomentsforkids.com

Find more books from our BeginningMind Series or our Pearl Collection, educating hearts and minds on http://shortmomentsforkids.com
Sign up to our email list to get a free ebook!

You are very welcome to leave a review.
They help others discover the gems of short moments in their life.

On our website you will find readalouds, a blog about supporting children to rely on strong mind with their stormy feelings and info about our weekly Dzogchen zoom classes for kids.

Socials @short_moments_for_kids

Printed in Great Britain
by Amazon